101 THINGS TO CHEER UP SUPPORTERS OF TERRIBLE FOOTBALL TEAMS

First published in 2023 by Allsorted Ltd WD19 4BG U.K.

ISBN 9781915902191

Printed in Croatia.

101 THINGS TO CHEER UP SUPPORTERS OF TERRIBLE FOOTBALL TEAMS

INTRODUCTION

In the world of football, it's not always a winning streak. Sometimes, your team might be at the wrong end of the league, and you need a bit of a pick-me-up. Enter '**101 Things to Cheer Up Supporters of Terrible Football Teams**'. This whimsical, light-hearted collection of trivia, quotes and anecdotes is sure to bring a smile to even the most disappointed fan's face. It's a gentle reminder that football isn't just about winning or losing—it's about passion, camaraderie, and sometimes, just a good laugh.

WHEN YOU'RE 4-0
UP YOU SHOULD NEVER
LOSE 7-1.

LAWRIE MCMENEMY

CONTRACT CLAUSES

Ronaldinho (Flamengo): Ronaldinho's 'nightclub clause' allowed him to party two nights per week.

Spencer Prior (Cardiff City): Prior was required to eat sheep's testicles as part of a contract-signing initiation.

Stefan Schwarz (Sunderland): Schwarz's contract prohibited him from travelling to space during his tenure.

Neil Ruddock (Crystal Palace): Ruddock had to maintain a specific weight to receive his full wage.

BIGGEST LOSING MARGIN IN AN INTERNATIONAL MATCH

The **Australian** national team beat **American Samoa** 31–0 in a Word Cup qualifier in 2021, marking the biggest win in an international match.

WINLESS STREAK BROKEN FOR 'UK'S WORST TEAM'

On 31 July 2019 **Fort William FC**, once dubbed the 'UK's worst professional football team', finally broke their 73-match winless streak. This came after a season that saw them suffer a dismal goal difference of 221.

SENT OFF FOR BREAKING WIND

In a unique case from the Swedish lower leagues in 2016, a player named **Ljungkvist** received a red card during a match between Järna SK and Pershagen SK. The cause of his dismissal was not for a foul or unsportsmanlike conduct of a traditional nature, but for loudly breaking wind near the referee. This led to a second yellow card, and consequently, a red card, with the referee deeming it as unsportsmanlike behaviour. The incident became a humorous anecdote in football lore.

FIRST RECORDED LOSS IN WOMEN'S FOOTBALL

In the historical 1895 match, the first recorded women's football game, the **southern team** suffered a resounding defeat. Despite their efforts, they lost to the **northern team** 7–1, marking this event as the first documented loss in women's football history.

WOLFGANG WOLF MANAGES WOLFSBURG

Football sometimes provides moments that feel destined. One such moment was when **Wolfgang Wolf** took over the managerial position at VfL Wolfsburg. Given that Wolf's last name and the club's name share the same root, this was a pairing that seemed fated to happen. Wolf managed the club from 1998 to 2003.

NAMES OF STADIUMS

Middelfart Stadium: Middelfart, Denmark

Hunky Dorys Park: Drogheda, Ireland (named after a sponsorship deal with a local snack food company)

Tony Macaroni Arena: Livingston, Scotland (named after a sponsorship deal with an Italian restaurant chain)

SUPERSTITIONS

Sergio Goycochea (Argentina): Goycochea urinated on the pitch for penalty-shootout luck in the 1990 World Cup.

Gary Lineker (England): Lineker avoided shooting pre-match to 'save goals'.

John Terry (Chelsea/England): Always used the same urinal.

Kolo Toure (Arsenal/Manchester City/Liverpool): Toure had the ritual of entering the pitch last.

Laurent Blanc (France): Blanc kissed goalkeeper Fabien Barthez's bald head before matches in the 1998 World Cup.

FINES

Robbie Savage (Leicester City): Savage was fined for using the referee's toilet during a match, which was against regulations.

Edgar Davids (Barnet): As player–manager, Davids substituted and fined himself after receiving a red card in a match.

Liam Ridgewell (West Bromwich Albion): Ridgewell was fined for a controversial photograph of him using money as toilet paper.

"LOSING IS NATURE'S WAY OF SAYING YOU NEED TO PRACTISE MORE."

ANONYMOUS

WEST BROMWICH STROLLERS

West Bromwich Albion FC (England): West Bromwich Albion FC was founded in 1878 by workers from the Salter's Spring Works, a factory that manufactured industrial springs. The club was initially named West Bromwich Strollers because the workers would 'stroll' to their matches. The name was eventually changed to West Bromwich Albion in 1880 to reflect their connection to the West Bromwich area.

CLUB NAMES

FC Santa Claus (Finland)

Deportivo Wanka (Peru)

The Strongest (Bolivia)

Fotballaget Fart (Norway)

INJURIES

Kevin Kyle (Sunderland/Scotland): Kyle burned his groin heating baby milk.

Darren Barnard (Barnsley/Wales): Barnard injured his knee slipping on puppy urine.

Kasey Keller (Leicester/USA): Keller broke his jaw taking his golf clubs out of his car boot.

Chic Brodie (Brentford): Brodie shattered his kneecap and ended his career after a collision with a dog.

Alex Stepney (Manchester United): Stepney dislocated his jaw yelling at defenders.

JOBS AFTER FOOTBALL

Faustino Asprilla: The former Colombian striker started his own brand of fruit-flavoured condoms.

Gavin Peacock: The midfielder became a pastor after hanging up his boots.

Curtis Woodhouse: The former Sheffield United and Birmingham City midfielder embarked on a boxing career after his football career ended. He later became the British light-welterweight champion.

Djibril Cisse: The former Liverpool and French national team striker pursued a career as a DJ and fashion designer after retiring from football.

Dion Dublin: The former Manchester United and Aston Villa striker invented a percussion instrument called 'The Dube' after retiring.

"LOSING WITH GRACE IS
OVERRATED. I PREFER
DRAMATIC SULKING."

ANONYMOUS

GOALKEEPERS SENT OFF IN WORLD CUP

Gianluca Pagliuca of Italy (1994) and **Itumeleng Khune** of South Africa (2010) hold the unique distinction of being the first goalkeepers sent off during World Cup tournaments.

OLDEST FOOTBALL CLUB

The world's oldest football club is England's **Sheffield F.C.**, founded in 1857. The club was established by Nathaniel Creswick and William Prest, who also created the "Sheffield Rules" which became a major influence on the modern rules of football.

A VERY FAST RED CARD

Cross Farm Park Celtic's **Lee Todd** received the quickest red card in history in 2000, just two seconds into the game. Todd was sent off saying 'F*** me, that was loud' in response to the referee's whistle, earning him an immediate dismissal for foul language.

MOST OWN GOALS

In 2002, **AS Adema of Madagascar** defeated SOE l'Emyrne 149–0 in a match where all 149 goals were own goals. The SOE l'Emyrne players intentionally scored own goals as a protest against a refereeing decision in a previous game.

ANIMAL PITCH INVASIONS

Pine Marten Chaos: A Swiss Super League game saw a pine marten invade the field, even biting a player before being caught by the goalkeeper.

Bees Swarm Goalpost: A 2017 Copa Libertadores match faced a 40-minute delay as firefighters removed thousands of bees from a goalpost.

Doggy Goalkeeper: A dog sprinted onto the field and accidentally saved a goal during a 2018 Argentine third-tier league match.

FOOTBALLERS' NAMES

Danny Invincibile: Australian footballer

Norman Conquest: Australian footballer

Danger Fourpence: Zimbabwean footballer

Creedence Clearwater Couto: Brazilian footballer

Wolfgang Wolf: German footballer and manager

Have-a-Look Dube: Zimbabwean footballer

Johnny Moustache: Seychellois footballer

QUICK SUBSTITUTION

Club manager **Dan Petrescu** made headlines when he substituted Alin Fica just 24 seconds into a game against Gaz Metan Media.

A VERY FITTING NAME

Nettie Honeyball, a fittingly named pioneer, sweetly shook societal norms by founding the British Ladies' Football Club in 1894. Her impact dribbled through history, breaking barriers in women's football.

"WE MUST HAVE HAD 99% OF THE GAME. IT WAS THE OTHER 3% THAT COST US THE MATCH."

RUUD GULLIT

THE WORLD'S OLDEST FOOTBALL

The world's oldest football still in existence was found in the rafters of **Stirling Castle** in Scotland. It's made of a pig's bladder covered in cow leather and dates back to the 1540s. The ball is now displayed at the Smith Art Gallery and Museum in Stirling, Scotland.

FIRST PAIR OF FOOTBALL BOOTS

The first specialised football boots were reportedly crafted for England's **King Henry VIII** in 1526. His personal shoemaker, Cornelius Johnson, made them from heavy, durable leather. These ankle-high boots were significantly sturdier than typical shoes of that period.

UNPRECEDENTED TWO-TEAM FOOTBALL LEAGUE

The Isles of Scilly Football League uniquely features only two teams: the **Woolpack Wanderers** and **Garrison Gunners**. These teams contest 18 games per season, alongside two annual cup competitions and a Charity Shield-style exhibition match.

"I SCORED A WORLDIE BUT THE ONLY WITNESS WAS POMPEY THE DOG."

TOM MAGGIE,
BUNGAY TOWN ROVERS

FIRST FIVE TEAMS TO LOSE IN THE WOMEN'S WORLD CUP FINAL

Norway 1991

Germany 1995

China PR 1999

Sweden 2003

Brazil 2007

ALI DIA: FOOTBALL'S GREATEST HOAX

In 1996, **Ali Dia**, dubbed 'Bambi on Ice', successfully tricked Southampton into believing he was a professional footballer. He was introduced to the team by someone impersonating FIFA World Player of the Year, George Weah, claiming Dia was his cousin and a Senegalese international. Signed on a one-month contract, Dia made only one disastrous appearance against Leeds United, replacing injured Matthew Le Tissier, and was promptly substituted. Dia was released after 14 days and managed to play for non-league Gateshead. Despite the scandal, Dia maintains he had a legitimate football career prior to this infamous incident.

WOMEN'S WORLD CUP TRAILBLAZERS

There are three nations whose women's teams have qualified for the World Cup whilst the men's teams didn't.

Taiwan (Chinese Taipei): They participated in the 1991 FIFA Women's World Cup.

Thailand: Their women's team participated in the FIFA Women's World Cup in 2015 and 2019.

Equatorial Guinea: Their women's team participated in the FIFA Women's World Cup in 2011 and 2015.

"IN FOOTBALL,
EVERYTHING IS
COMPLICATED BY THE
PRESENCE OF THE
OPPOSITE TEAM."

JEAN-PAUL SARTRE

HEREFORD'S DAVID VS GOLIATH VICTORY

In a shocking upset, **Hereford United** defeated top-flight team **Newcastle United** in the third round of the 1972 FA Cup. After extra time, Hereford United emerged victorious with a 2–1 scoreline.

THE WORST PREMIER LEAGUE SEASON

The worst Premier League season on record in terms of points achieved is held by **Derby County** during the 2007–08 season. They finished the season with just 11 points from 38 matches, which is the lowest total in the history of the Premier League.

OWN GOAL KING

Richard Dunne scored 10 own goals in his Premier League career.

HOW DID THE FOOTBALL PITCH GET WET?

THE PLAYERS DRIBBLED ALL OVER IT.

RED CARD MADNESS

A Brazilian league match between **Vitoria** and **Bahia** in 2018 saw the record for the highest number of red cards in a single match, with the referee showing 10 red cards, evenly split between the teams, following a mass brawl. The match was subsequently abandoned.

HULL CITY'S UNIQUE TYPOGRAPHY QUIRK

Hull City stand alone in the Football League with a unique typographical distinction – it's the only team where none of the letters in its name can be coloured in.

WHICH FOOTBALL TEAM USES THE MOST TOILET PAPER?

YOU CAN WORK THAT OUT FOR YOURSELF!

"MY PARTNER HAS JUST LEFT ME. THEY SAID MY LIFE REVOLVED AROUND FOOTBALL AND THEY WERE SICK OF IT. I'M QUITE UPSET. WE WERE TOGETHER FOR SEVEN SEASONS."

ANONYMOUS

RECORD FOR MOST CLUBS MANAGED BY A SINGLE MANAGER

The German football manager **Rudi Gutendorf** earned the nickname 'Restless Rudi' due to the extensive breadth of his career. Over his lifetime, Gutendorf managed 55 different clubs.

BATTLE OF NUREMBERG

In the 2006 FIFA World Cup quarter-final match between **Portugal** and the **Netherlands**, the match was so rough and ill-disciplined that it's known as the 'Battle of Nuremberg'. The referee issued a record-breaking 16 yellow cards and 4 red cards during the game.

AMERICA NOT TO BLAME FOR TERM 'SOCCER'

Although many people blame America for the change in the name from football to soccer, the term 'soccer' was first used in England to distinguish the game from rugby. It is short for 'association football'.

SOLD BY FIANCÉE

Paul Peschisolido's transfer from Birmingham City to Stoke City in 1994 was unique. His then fiancée and Managing Director of Birmingham City, Karren Brady, sold him in a £400,000 deal.

BALL HITS ALL THREE POSTS

In a 2016 UEFA Europa League match between **Rapid Vienna** and **Viktoria Plzen**, Rapid Vienna's Matej Jelic accomplished a rare feat. His shot hit both goalposts and the crossbar before finally going in.

WHY WAS THE BEST
FOOTBALLER IN THE
WORLD ASKED TO TIDY
HIS ROOM?

BECAUSE HE WAS MESSI.

JOMO SONO'S WEDDING DAY TURNAROUND

Ephraim 'Jomo' Sono achieved something extraordinary on his wedding day. After leaving his own ceremony, Sono came on as a substitute for his Orlando Pirates team, which was down 2–0 at half-time. He assisted three goals, scored one, and led his team to a 4–2 victory, before returning to his wedding reception.

REFEREE'S TRIPLE YELLOW CARD GAFFE

During a 2006 FIFA World Cup match, English referee **Graham Poll** made a remarkable blunder. He showed Croatia's Josip Šimunić three yellow cards before sending him off, violating the rule that a player should be sent off after two yellow cards.

"FAILURE HAPPENS ALL THE TIME, IT HAPPENS EVERYDAY IN PRACTICE, WHAT MAKES YOU BETTER IS HOW YOU REACT TO IT."

MIA HAMM

LATVIA LOSE TO ENGLAND'S LIONESSES 20–0

On 30 November 2021, **England's Lionesses** recorded their biggest ever win, by thrashing Latvia 20–0 in a World Cup qualifier. Three players scored hat-tricks, leading to a hat-trick of hat-tricks.

"WE ARE ON A STRICT RUNNING REGIME: WE RUN THE RISK OF LOSING EVERY GAME."

ANONYMOUS

GERMANY WORLD CUP FINALS

Germany's national football team has experienced its share of heartbreak on the biggest stage in football, having lost four World Cup finals. These occurred in the years 1966, 1982, 1986, and 2002.

ALEX SONG'S SIBLINGS

The football world is full of interesting personal stories, and former Arsenal and Barcelona player **Alex Song** is no exception. Known for his skill on the pitch, Song also stands out for his large family. He is one of 28 siblings, with 17 sisters and 10 brothers.

"I WOULD NOT BE BOTHERED IF WE LOST EVERY GAME AS LONG AS WE WON THE LEAGUE."

MARK VIDUKA

MARK HUGHES' DOUBLE DUTY

There are few days in a footballer's life as eventful as the one **Mark Hughes** had in 1987. The Welsh striker played for his national team against Czechoslovakia in Prague in the morning, then boarded a plane, and by afternoon was playing for his club, Bayern Munich.

WEST BROMWICH ALBION'S NAMING PATTERN

Between 1975 and 1988, **West Bromwich Albion's** managerial appointments seemed to follow a peculiar naming pattern. The club's managers during this period were named **Johnny**, **Ronnie**, **John**, **Ron**, **Ronnie**, **Ron**, **Johnny**, **Nobby**, **Ron** and **Ron**!

"REFEREEING IN THE SUNDAY LEAGUE IS LIKE TRYING TO CONTROL TRAFFIC... BLINDFOLDED!"

ANONYMOUS

CHICKEN INVASION

In 2012, a chicken dressed in a **Blackburn Rovers** flag was let loose onto the pitch during their game against Wigan Athletic. The chicken, a symbol of the club's owners Venky's who are an Indian company specialising in chicken meat processing, was a protest from the Blackburn fans who were unhappy with the management of their club.

WHAT DO YOU CALL A
FOOTBALLER WHO BRINGS
A LENGTH OF ROPE ONTO
THE FOOTBALL PITCH?

THE SKIPPER.

RYAN GIGGS' PROLIFIC SCORING RECORD WITHOUT A HAT-TRICK

Welsh footballer **Ryan Giggs** netted over one hundred goals during his glittering Manchester United career but astonishingly, never once scored a hat-trick. Despite his impressive tally and numerous match-winning performances, three goals in a single game eluded this footballing legend.

FIRST LOSERS IN FIFA WORLD CUP HISTORY: MEXICO AND BELGIUM

FIFA's inaugural World Cup took place in 1930 in Uruguay. On the tournament's opening day, **Mexico** and **Belgium** became the first teams to taste defeat. Mexico lost 4–1 to France, and Belgium were beaten 3–0 by the United States, etching their names in the history books for this unwanted record.

"WE DIDN'T LOSE THE GAME, WE JUST RAN OUT OF TIME."

VINCE LOMBARDI

RED CARDS AT CRUCIAL MOMENTS

Zinedine Zidane's (France) headbutt in the 2006 World Cup final

Luis Suarez's (Uruguay) deliberate handball in 2010 World Cup quarter final

David Beckham's (England) kick in 1998 World Cup knockout phase

UEFA PRESIDENT'S LIFT MISHAP

Lennart Johansson, UEFA President, experienced a mishap during the 1999 Champions League final. While in the stadium lift, he missed Manchester United's crucial last-minute comeback goals!

FEWEST FANS AT A GAME

The smallest-ever crowd for a match in the English Football League was just 13 spectators, for **Stockport County's** game against **Leicester City** in 1921.

ROMANIA'S BLOND AMBITION AT THE 1998 WORLD CUP

During the 1998 World Cup, the **Romanian** national football team added an unexpected twist to the tournament. After a surprising win against England in the group stages, the players decided to dye their hair blond as a symbol of unity and to boost team morale. The bold, unifying move drew international attention and was a spirited attempt to further their success in the tournament. However, despite their striking new look and enhanced team spirit, they met with disappointment when they faced Croatia. The Croatian team outwitted them, ending their World Cup run and proving that while hair dye might change appearances, it doesn't necessarily translate into winning goals.

"THERE'S NO I IN TEAM,
BUT THERE'S ONE IN
'I THINK WE'RE GOING
TO LOSE'."

ANONYMOUS

TRAFFIC LIGHTS INSPIRE
FOOTBALL'S CARD SYSTEM

British referee **Ken Aston** conceived the idea of
the yellow and red card system while driving in
London. The changing traffic lights sparked the
concept of a universally understood disciplinary
system for football, which was implemented in
the 1970 FIFA World Cup.

ZLATAN IBRAHIMOVIC NEVER WON CHAMPIONS LEAGUE

Zlatan Ibrahimovic has played for six clubs that have won the Champions League, but he has never actually won the trophy himself. The striker has been at Ajax, Barcelona, Inter, Juventus, Milan and Manchester United.

"I'VE GOT THE TURNING SPEED OF A CARGO SHIP AND THE FITNESS OF A RETIRED SNAIL."

ANONYMOUS

"IF LOSING BUILDS CHARACTER, THEN WE ARE DUE FOR A LEAD ROLE IN A BLOCKBUSTER."

HUGO CHADD,
DITCHINGHAM DODGERS

FIRST COOLING BREAK
IN WORLD CUP HISTORY

The match between the **Netherlands** and **Mexico** on 29 June 2014, was played in extreme heat reaching up to 39°C (102°F). This match is noteworthy as it was the first time that official cooling breaks were introduced in a World Cup tournament.

"SUCCESS IS GOING
FROM FAILURE TO
FAILURE WITHOUT LOSING
ENTHUSIASM."

WINSTON CHURCHILL

ASTON VILLA MORE SUCCESSFUL THAN MANCHESTER UNITED

Before the arrival of **Sir Alex Ferguson** at Manchester United in 1986, Aston Villa held an edge over the Red Devils in terms of major football honours. Aston Villa had won an impressive array of trophies: seven league titles, seven FA Cups, three League Cups, and the prestigious European Cup.

2006 WORLD CUP'S RECORD FOR HIGHEST NUMBER OF RED CARDS

The **2006 World Cup** holds the record for the highest number of red cards issued in a single tournament. During the competition, a total of 28 players were sent off, adding a significant level of drama and tension to the matches.

HAT-TRICK AGAINST THREE DIFFERENT GOALKEEPERS

In a unique 1986 match, West Ham's **Alvin Martin** scored a hat-trick against three different Newcastle goalkeepers. His targets included regular goalkeeper Martin Thomas, defender Chris Hedworth who stepped in, and eventually Peter Beardsley. West Ham triumphed with an 8–1 victory.

THE GREATEST PLAYER
WHO NEVER PLAYED

Brazilian footballer **Carlos Kaiser** managed to have a professional career spanning nearly two decades, all without actually playing a game. He used fake injuries to avoid playing and smooth talking to keep getting contracts!

"WE'VE LEARNED SO MUCH FROM LOSSES. WE THINK WE'LL LEARN SOME MORE."

ANONYMOUS

OLDEST WORLD CUP GOAL SCORER ROGER MILLA'S RECORD

Cameroon's Roger Milla, at the ripe old age of 42 years and 39 days, scored a goal against Russia during the 1994 World Cup. His feat makes him the oldest goal scorer in the history of the tournament.

MOST WORLD CUP FINALS
WITHOUT A WIN

The Netherlands have reached three World Cup finals (1974, 1978, 2010) but have never won the tournament, marking the longest time a team has gone without winning the World Cup after reaching the final.

SPAIN'S LOW-SCORING WORLD CUP TRIUMPH

Spain achieved an incredible feat by winning the World Cup with just eight goals, the lowest tally ever scored by a championship-winning team.

"THE MORE DIFFICULT
THE VICTORY, THE
GREATER THE HAPPINESS
IN WINNING."

PELE

"It's not about winning or losing, it's about how you blame the other team."

Anonymous

MOST GOALS SCORED BY A SUBSTITUTE IN A PREMIER LEAGUE MATCH

Ole Gunnar Solskjær, playing for Manchester United, scored four goals as a substitute in a single Premier League match against Nottingham Forest in 1999.

TWINS FOR DIFFERENT COUNTRIES

The Boateng brothers, **Kevin-Prince** and **Jerome**, are one of the few sets of brothers to have represented different nations at the World Cup. Kevin-Prince chose to represent Ghana, while Jerome played for Germany.

FIRST PREMIER LEAGUE MANAGER SACKED

Ian Porterfield was the first manager to be sacked in the Premier League era after a poor performance by Chelsea in the 1993–94 season.

"THE BABE IS HERE. WHO'S COMING IN SECOND?"

BABE DIDRIKSON ZAHARIAS

WHAT DID THE FOOTBALLER GET FOR HER BIRTHDAY?

A RED CARD.

SUPER CALEY GO BALLISTIC, CELTIC ARE ATROCIOUS

In 1999, **Inverness Caledonian Thistle** beat **Celtic** 3–1 in the Scottish Cup. The match was so shocking that a newspaper headline famously read 'Super Caley Go Ballistic, Celtic Are Atrocious'.

UNINTENDED HAT-TRICK

Chris Nicholl, while playing for Aston Villa against Leicester City in 1976, accomplished a rare feat by scoring all four goals in a 2–2 draw. This included two goals for his own team and two own goals, giving him a unique place in football history.

1950 US TEAM:
THE DAY-JOB WORLD CUP HEROES

In the 1950 World Cup, the **US team** that defeated England 1–0 comprised players who had regular day jobs, from a postman and a hearse driver, to a dish-washer and a teacher. This win against England remains one of the biggest upsets in World Cup history.

"FOOTBALL IS A SIMPLE GAME. TWENTY-TWO MEN CHASE A BALL FOR 90 MINUTES AND AT THE END, THE GERMANS ALWAYS WIN."

GARY LINEKER

WHAT DOES AN ENGLAND FAN DO AFTER WINNING A MAJOR TOURNAMENT?

TURN OFF THE XBOX.

A VERY RAPID DECLINE

After finishing eighth in the Premier League, **Portsmouth Football Club** experienced a sharp fall from grace, suffering three relegations in four seasons – from Premier League to League Two, the fourth tier of English football. This dramatic descent included relegation from the Premier League (2009–10), Championship (2011–12), and League One (2012–13).

FASTEST DISMISSAL AFTER COMING ON AS A SUBSTITUTE

Walter Boyd of Swansea City holds this dubious record. He was sent off in 2000 for violent conduct just seconds after coming on as a substitute.

WHAT'S THE WORST THING THAT CAN HAPPEN TO A FOOTBALL PLAYER?

TO HAVE NO GOAL IN LIFE.

ANDY HESSENTHALER'S MANAGER—PLAYER TRICK

As player–manager for Gillingham, **Andy Hessenthaler** found a unique workaround when he was red-carded while managing a match against Cardiff. He substituted himself on as a player, exploiting a loophole in the rules.

"IF AT FIRST YOU DON'T
SUCCEED, TRY, TRY
AGAIN. THEN QUIT.
THERE'S NO POINT IN
BEING A DAMN FOOL
ABOUT IT."

W.C. FIELDS

ARSENAL'S EPIC UNBEATEN RUN BROKEN

Arsenal's record-breaking unbeaten streak of 49 matches in the English Premier League, which spanned from May 2003 to October 2004, was finally ended by Manchester United. Manchester United won the game 2-0 at their home ground, Old Trafford.

"SOMETIMES IN FOOTBALL, YOU HAVE TO HOLD YOUR HAND UP AND SAY, YEAH, THEY'RE BETTER THAN US."

ALEX FERGUSON